T0407737

SCORPION

BY RACHEL HAMBY

Apex is distributed by North Star Editions:
sales@northstareditions.com | 888-417-0195

Produced for Apex by Red Line Editorial.

Photographs ©: Shutterstock Images, cover, 1, 4–5, 6–7, 8, 8–9, 10–11, 12, 13, 14–15, 16–17, 18, 19, 20, 22–23, 24–25, 26–27, 29

Library of Congress Control Number: 2022901419

ISBN
978-1-63738-286-8 (hardcover)
978-1-63738-322-3 (paperback)
978-1-63738-393-3 (ebook pdf)
978-1-63738-358-2 (hosted ebook)

Printed in the United States of America
Mankato, MN
082022

NOTE TO PARENTS AND EDUCATORS

Apex books are designed to build literacy skills in striving readers. Exciting, high-interest content attracts and holds readers' attention. The text is carefully leveled to allow students to achieve success quickly. Additional features, such as bolded glossary words for difficult terms, help build comprehension.

TABLE OF CONTENTS

CHAPTER 1

A SCORPION'S STING

A scorpion sits in the dark. It is hunting for **prey**. Soon, a spider walks by. The scorpion runs toward it.

Scorpions often hide and wait for prey.

A SHARP STINGER

A scorpion's stinger is at the end of its tail. The stinger is hollow. Poison runs through it. Scorpions can bend and twist their tails to sting prey.

The scorpion catches the spider with its **pincers**. It jabs its stinger into the spider's body. The stinger releases poison. The poison kills the spider.

A scorpion's tail is long and curved.

Next, the scorpion spits on its food. The spit breaks the food down to mush. Then, the scorpion slurps it up.

Scorpions spit stomach juices onto their food before eating it.

Deathstalker scorpions live in deserts in North Africa and the Middle East.

CHAPTER 2

THE LiFE OF A SCORPiON

There are about 1,500 scorpion **species**. They can be found in many places around the world. Many live in **deserts**. Others live in grasslands, **rain forests**, or caves.

Emperor scorpions live in rain forests in West Africa.

Scorpions range in size. They can also be many colors. Their colors help them blend in with their surroundings.

Scorpions can be brown, black, red, green, blue, or yellow.

The giant forest scorpion lives in Asia. It's the world's largest scorpion.

FAST FACT

The largest scorpion is more than 9 inches (23 cm) long. The smallest is only 0.5 inches (1 cm) long.

Some scorpions dig small holes each day. Others make deep holes to use many times.

Scorpions dig holes in the ground. They hide in these holes. That way, they stay safe and cool. At night, scorpions come out to hunt.

FINDING FOSSILS

Scientists study scorpion fossils. Some of these fossils are 420 million years old. They show that scorpions lived on Earth before dinosaurs did.

CHAPTER 3

A SCORPION'S BODY

Scorpions have eight legs. They also have two pincers. The pincers look like claws. Scorpions use them to grab prey.

A scorpion's pincers are part of its mouth.

As they grow, scorpions shed their old exoskeletons and grow new ones.

A scorpion doesn't have bones. Instead, it has a hard **exoskeleton**. The exoskeleton covers its body. It protects the scorpion from **predators**.

BABY SCORPIONS

Scorpions are born with soft bodies. Their exoskeletons harden in one to two weeks. Until then, baby scorpions ride on their mother's back. She helps keep them safe.

A female scorpion can have up to 100 babies at a time.

Scorpions have several pairs of eyes. But they don't see very well. They rely on their senses of touch and hearing instead.

FAST FACT

A scorpion's body is covered in tiny hairs. They help the scorpion sense movement.

CHAPTER 4

ON THE HUNT

Scorpions eat meat. Their prey includes insects, lizards, and mice. Scorpions may crush small prey with their pincers.

Some scorpions can go a year without food after they eat one bug.

SLOW EATERS

Scorpions do not have teeth. They use their pincers to tear up their food. They may take up to an hour to eat one meal.

A marbled scorpion's sting is painful. Other scorpion species can be deadly.

A scorpion stings large or fast-moving prey. Its poison makes the prey unable to move. The prey can't breathe. Its heart stops. It dies.

Scorpions may also sting to protect themselves. More than one million people get stung by scorpions each year. Most of those people survive. But some scorpions' poison can kill humans.

Some types of birds eat scorpions. Other predators include bats and lizards.

27

COMPREHENSION QUESTIONS

Write your answers on a separate piece of paper.

1. Write a few sentences describing how a scorpion eats.

2. Do you think a scorpion would make a good pet? Why or why not?

3. Which body part helps a scorpion sense movement?

> **A.** its pincers
>
> **B.** its stinger
>
> **C.** hairs on its body

4. Why would hiding in holes help scorpions stay cool?

> **A.** The holes help scorpions find more food.
>
> **B.** The holes help scorpions get more sunlight.
>
> **C.** The holes keep the scorpions out of the hot sun.

5. What does **protects** mean in this book?

The exoskeleton covers its body. It protects the scorpion from predators.

  A. shows something off
  B. keeps something safe
  C. keeps something warm

6. What does **deadliest** mean in this book?

The deathstalker is one of the world's deadliest scorpions. Its poison can kill humans.

  A. very slow moving
  B. most likely to hide
  C. most likely to kill

Answer key on page 32.

GLOSSARY

deserts
Areas of land that have few plants and get very little rain.

exoskeleton
A hard covering that protects the body.

fossils
Remains of plants and animals that lived long ago.

hollow
Having empty space inside.

pincers
Claw-like body parts that open and close to grab or pinch.

predators
Animals that hunt and eat other animals.

prey
An animal that is hunted and eaten by another animal.

rain forests
Areas with many trees and lots of rain.

species
Groups of animals or plants that are similar and can breed with one another.

TO LEARN MORE

BOOKS

Adamson, Thomas K. *Scorpion vs. Tarantula*. Minneapolis: Bellwether Media, 2021.

Bridges, Melanie, and Camilla de la Bédoyère. *Scary Bugs*. London: Quarto Publishing Group, 2019.

Sirota, Lyn. *Scorpions*. Mankato, MN: Black Rabbit Books, 2020.

ONLINE RESOURCES

Visit **www.apexeditions.com** to find links and resources related to this title.

ABOUT THE AUTHOR

Rachel Hamby writes poetry, fiction, and nonfiction for young readers. She lives in Washington State with her husband, kids, and corgis.

INDEX

ANSWER KEY:
1. Answers will vary; 2. Answers will vary; 3. C; 4. C; 5. B; 6. C